HOW TO START YOUR BUSINESS IN THE UNITED STATES

Create Your U.S. Company in Delaware or Elsewhere in the USA

VINCENT ALLARD

CorpoMax

Publisher
CorpoMax Publishing LLC

Cover Design
Marie-Andrée Lemieux - malem.com

Cover Image
© dvarg - 123rf.com

ISBN
E-book ISBN: 978-1-952012-09-9
Paperback ISBN: 978-1-952012-03-7

Edition
First Edition

Series
First book in the YES TO ENTREPRENEURS® series

WHAT THEY SAY

“Simple. Clear. Precise. Complete. Reading Vincent Allard is having a great time, with a friend who gives us, without pontificating, the best advice to help us succeed in setting up a business in the USA. Cartesian, he divides the challenge into three parts, three books, to properly analyze, explain and better solve difficulties. A must.”

Richard JOHNSON, Retired Journalist, Journal of Montreal

“Books such as those in the *Yes to Entrepreneurs* series provide businesses with useful information and practical tools to expand into the United States market, the largest consumer market and recipient of foreign direct investment in the world.”

Gina BENTO, Commercial Specialist, U.S. Department of Commerce, International Trade Administration

“Never before have guides been so deserving of the term *practical*! With his trilogy, Vincent Allard offers us in a controlled, organized, complete, but also airy and digestible way everything there is to know about setting up a business in the United States, its name and its banking management. I keep these books on my desk, within easy reach. That is how useful they are.”

Bernard GEENEN, Economic and Commercial Counselor, Wallonia Export & Investment Agency, Consulate of Belgium, New York

“I received and read carefully the three guides by Vincent Allard, lawyer and founder of CorpoMax. I am delighted because it is an undeniable help for any entrepreneur who wants to start a business in the United States. It's simple, you are guided and you can feel Vincent Allard's great experience through his advice and recommendations. Also for the legal practitioner, it is a source to many questions that our French and European clients ask us. Congratulations again and thank you!"

Isabelle LANDREAU, Lawyer of the Paris Bar, Founder of Smart Law Fabrik

"My business is advising emerging Canadian companies on developing their business in the United States. I have been doing that for a long time. The aspects of incorporation, setting up bank accounts, even choice of name for doing business in the U.S. can seem complicated. But these guides are great. Everything you need to do is spelled out simply and directly, requirement by requirement, issue by issue. They are ideal for entrepreneurs looking to do business in the United States. Easy to read and to the point. Everything basic that is involved is clearly laid out. I highly recommend their use."

Tom CREARY, Managing Director of WestbridgeOne Consulting, Founder and Past Chairman of the American Chamber of Commerce in Canada - Quebec Chapter

"The *Yes to Entrepreneurs* book series is extremely structured, complete and easy to use, like the services offered by CorpoMax. This solid and valuable work greatly simplifies the task of entrepreneurs, advisers and lawyers. It adds value to our advice and makes the American dream very accessible. We wish this collection a long life and thank Vincent Allard for his permanent dedication."

Serge BOUGANIM, Lawyer of the Paris and Brussels Bars

"Finally a practical and clear guide to answer the questions that any entrepreneur wishing to create a business in the United States is asking !!! The success of an establishment depends above all on good knowledge of the rules of law but also of local commercial practices. In this respect, the corporate name of the company is crucial and the practical advice given by Mr. Allard in his work is particularly relevant and useful. In general, the three books published by Mr. Allard provide a better understanding of the legal issues related to setting up a business in the United States and will help entrepreneurs in carrying out their project."

François BOSCHER, Lawyer of the Tours Bar (1981-1992) and the Quebec Bar (1995- ...), Former President of the French Chamber of Commerce and Industry in Canada - CCIFC

"Congratulations to my colleague Vincent Allard for the publication of three exceptional popularization books for entrepreneurs who want to start a business in the United States. Reference books, advice books, more than 600 pages that guide us in the land of Uncle Sam to get the best results."

Pierre CHAGNON, Retired Emeritus Attorney, Bâtonnier of Quebec

"As someone new to American business, there is so much information, on-line, consultants, advisors, it's all very intimidating. Tell it to me straight... and at last we have it! In easy and amusing terms that gave me confidence in making the right choice, to start my business in America."

Captain Peter FABIAN (ret.), CEO, Advanced Coatings Engineering LLC

"A master at simplifying complex information for all to understand, Vincent Allard has succeeded in putting together a concise, well written and easy to read series on starting a business in the United States. The *Yes to Entrepreneurs* series takes you by the hand and guides you through the steps of incorporating a company, naming it appropriately and even starting a bank account. This series is full of practical information and a must read for both legal professionals looking to gain knowledge in basic American corporate legal issues, and for the motivated entrepreneurs looking to get one step closer to living the American dream."

George VARDATSIKOS, Ph.D.(med.), LL.L., Attorney of the Quebec Bar

"This series of practical guides allows entrepreneurs and professionals who advise them to benefit from the experience of thousands of other entrepreneurs who have started their business in the United States. There are a lot of details that could help their own business."

Robert CHAYER, U.S. Tax Expert, Canada

"Reading highly recommended. Three essential and very comprehensive guides for all immigrant candidates who wish to familiarize themselves with the important concepts to start their professional installation in the United States. These books are very well structured and expose in a very instructive way, but in a simple and accessible language, the concepts to know to make informed decisions concerning their American structure. From the corporate form to the choice of name, including tax implications, everything is there."

Estelle BERENBAUM, Immigration Lawyer, Florida

"Creating companies and doing business in the United States is a journey full of pitfalls. As a European, we underestimate the complexity of American law and its implications. Vincent Allard's Yes to Entrepreneurs collection provides ready-to-use pragmatic knowledge to successfully navigate American *waters*."

Arnaud LABOSSIÈRE, CEO, The Free Minds Press Ltd

"The information contained in Mr. Allard's trilogy of books will be extremely useful to any entrepreneur wishing to enter the U.S. market. The high quality of information is presented in a structured manner and is easily accessible, due to the author's great talent in simplifying complex matters."

Patric BESNER, Besner Business Lawyers

CONTENTS

EXCLUSIVE BONUS

Throughout the process of writing this guide, I accumulated many hyperlinks that greatly enrich its content.

An up-to-date list of these hyperlinks can be found at the web address listed in the *Useful Resources* section, at the end of this guide.

DEDICATION

I dedicate this practical guide to the thousands of entrepreneurs, from more than 50 countries, who have trusted CorpoMax since its foundation in 2001. Without them, CorpoMax would not exist.

PREFACE

Starting a business is not easy. Starting a business in a foreign country, even less so.

In 1998, I was a well-established lawyer in Montreal, Canada. I had hundreds of entrepreneurial clients, a stable family life, and quality friends. Everything to be happy. Except one day...

One day, I decided to immigrate to the United States. To sell my stake in my law firm. To sell the house. And to go with the family and our dog Rusty.

For the first two years after arriving in the United States, I worked for Jurifax, a contract forms publisher, which I co-founded in 1995.

Then, in 2001, I decided to launch CorpoMax, which specializes in the formation of U.S. companies.

Since the foundation of CorpoMax, several thousand entrepreneurs from more than 50 countries have trusted me. Thanks to these entrepreneurs, the entire CorpoMax team has been able to develop a unique expertise in the creation of U.S. companies.

Today, I would like to share with you the knowledge I have acquired over the past 20 years.

You are an entrepreneur yourself. You dream of starting your business in the United States, or setting up a subsidiary of your existing company on American soil. I sincerely believe that this practical guide will be very useful to you.

1 - INTRODUCTION

1.1 - PRESENTATION

Welcome to this practical guide on how to start your business in the United States.

My name is Vincent Allard. I am a business lawyer, but first and foremost an entrepreneur, who moved to the United States in 1999. For nearly 20 years, through my website corpomax.com, I have helped thousands of entrepreneurs from more than 50 countries start their businesses in the United States.

OBJECTIVES

This practical guide is mainly intended for you, a foreign entrepreneur who wants to create his or her American company.

This guide has two objectives.

Objective no. 1 is to give you a clear understanding of how your future company will work, in simple and clear language.

Objective no. 2 is to provide you with the tools you need to launch a successful company, despite the obstacles and distance.

PHASES

Together, we will explore the various phases of the life of your U.S. company.

First of all, we will focus on the creation of your company.

Then, we will discuss its domiciliation, real or virtual.

Next, we will consider the annual obligations of your company, especially at the corporate level.

Then, a few words on the taxation of your company, in broad terms, of course.

We will then analyze some corporate situations that may arise.

We will end with the closure of your company, voluntary or forced.

PRACTICAL GUIDE

Attention! This practical guide is not a legal, accounting, or tax guide. For this, you will need to consult professionals working in these areas.

This guide is essentially practical and contains many examples.

In short, this practical guide has been prepared for easy reading and immediate understanding.

I sincerely hope this practical guide will provide you with the information and inspiration you need to start your business in the United States.

If you have any questions, comments or suggestions about this guide, including its *Useful Resources* section, please feel free to contact me.

Thank you and good reading!

2 - WHERE TO CREATE YOUR U.S. COMPANY?

2.1 - IN GENERAL

We always talk about a U.S. company. But, basically, does it really exist? In France, we talk about a French company, because it was created by the French government. In Canada, we talk about a Canadian company, because it was created by the Canadian government. But in the United States, save for some rare exceptions, no companies are created at the federal level.

Instead, the right to create a company belongs to the 50 U.S. States and the District of Columbia. So, even though we talk about a U.S. company, in reality we should talk about a state company. For example, a company created in Delaware, a company created in Florida, or a company created in the state of New York. But, nevertheless, colloquially we talk about a U.S. company.

50 STATES

Fifty states – without counting the District of Columbia, it means:

- 50 corporate laws
- 50 sets of administrative rules

- 50 lists of government costs
- 50 time frames for the creation of companies
- 50 annual requirements

In short, it means 50 ways of doing things, sometimes very differently from one state to another.

Finally, here are three points you should remember.

1. PLACE OF CREATION

U.S. lawyers all agree: Do not choose the place where you will create your American company based on its proposed future location or because one state is more popular than another in a blog you have read.

2. LAWS AND TAXES

It is preferable to choose the place where you will create your U.S. company based on the quality of its corporate laws, the protection those laws give to shareholders and directors, and based on the tax benefits it provides.

3. SINGLE JURISDICTION

If several companies are involved, it is preferable to create them in the same jurisdiction. This will make any future merger or consolidation much easier.

2.2 - THE STATE OF DELAWARE AND ITS 15 SECRETS

What is Delaware? Delaware is one of the 50 U.S. states. It is located on the eastern coast of the United States, between New York City and Washington, D.C., the capital of the United States. The state of Delaware is the second smallest state, the first being Rhode Island.

Delaware is often referred to as *The First State*: it was the first state to sign the U.S. constitution in 1787.

But Delaware is best known for its 15 secrets. Let us discover them now.

1. INTERNATIONAL REPUTATION

Delegations from around the world come to Delaware to learn and understand the functioning of its corporate system, which is absolutely unique in the world.

2. PUBLIC RECORDS

Delaware's public records contain the name of the company, its legal form, the date of its creation, and the name and address of its registered agent.

However, these records do not contain the name or address of the company's shareholders, directors, or officers, unless this information was mentioned in the certificate of creation, which is rare. The absence of this information is particular to Delaware. In most states, the public records generally contain the name and address of the company's directors and officers.

3. INVESTMENT REQUIRED

Delaware does not require a minimum investment in the company. The shares need not have a par value, and a paid-up share capital of $1 is sufficient.

4. BANK ACCOUNT

A company created in Delaware has no obligation to have a bank account in this state. In fact, there is no obligation for a Delaware company to have a bank account in the United States. But it is normal and especially logical for a U.S. company to have a bank account on U.S. soil.

5. HEAD OFFICE

A company created in Delaware has no obligation to have its head office or principal place of business in the state. But what we often see is a head office in Delaware and a principal place of business in another state.

6. SHAREHOLDERS, DIRECTORS, AND OFFICERS

A single individual can be a shareholder, director, and officer of a Delaware company, all at the same time. The minimum is, therefore, one person. In addition, there is no obligation to reside in Delaware or even hold meetings there.

7. FREEDOM OF THE DIRECTORS

The directors of a company created in Delaware are free to establish the selling price of the company's shares. They can also adopt, amend, or repeal any of the company's by-laws. In other words, they have a lot of freedom.

8. CORPORATE INCOME TAX

If a Delaware company does not have a physical place of business in the state, it generally does not have to pay income tax in Delaware.

9. PERSONAL INCOME TAX AND SALES TAX

Generally, if a person holds shares of a Delaware company, but does not reside there, the person does not have to pay income tax in Delaware. In addition, Delaware does not have a sales tax.

10. SUCCESSION DUTIES

Generally, if a person holds shares of a Delaware company, but does not reside there, no succession duties are payable in Delaware when the person dies.

11. FAVORABLE LEGISLATION

Delaware has enacted a series of corporate laws that are favorable to companies and recognize the freedom to contract.

These laws are among the most advanced and flexible in the United States. The Delaware legislature constantly updates these laws in order to maintain their effectiveness.

12. SPECIALIZED COURTS

In Delaware, there is a specialized court in corporate law called the Court of Chancery. The Court relies on case law developed over more than 200 years, which insures a great deal of consistency in the decisions it makes.

13. CREATION COSTS AND ANNUAL TAX

The cost of creating a Delaware company is among the lowest in the United States. As for the annual corporate tax, it is comparable to the corporate tax paid elsewhere in the country.

14. SPEED OF CREATION

In Delaware, it is possible to create a company in just half an hour.

15. EASE OF CREATION

It is very easy to create a company in Delaware, especially when you use the services of an attorney or a firm specialized in the creation of U.S. companies.

~

Finally, here are three points you should remember.

1. WORLD RENOWNED

Since 2001, CorpoMax has incorporated thousands of companies throughout the United States. Although physically located in the state of Delaware, CorpoMax offers its incorporation services in all 50 states. In addition, CorpoMax has customers in over 50 countries. Nevertheless, 95 times out of 100, CorpoMax receives an order form requesting a Delaware company.

2. DIVISION OF CORPORATIONS

Delaware's Division of Corporations is a group of public servants fully dedicated to their mission. The Division is operational from 7 a.m. to midnight (8 a.m. to 5 p.m. for the public), Monday to Friday. On several occasions, I was able to talk to a public servant late at night. The Division is so efficient that it has obtained international ISO 9001 certification, proof of the excellence of its quality management system.

3. CERTIFICATE OF CREATION

It is generally not recommended to include the name of the shareholders, directors, or officers on the certificate of creation of a Delaware company. Indeed, with time, people leave or are replaced. It is therefore preferable to indicate this information in the corporate ledger rather than the certificate of creation.

2.3. - DELAWARE: STATISTICS AND EXAMPLES

The creation of companies in Delaware is a huge industry. To convince us, let us take a look at some incredible statistics.

STATISTICS

The Delaware register of companies lists:

- Over 50% of the U.S. public companies
- Over 67% of the Fortune 500 companies
- Over 50% of the companies listed on the New York Stock Exchange.

In 2019, 89% of IPOs - initial public offerings - were made by companies created in Delaware.

Also in 2019, the state created more than 226,000 new entities.

To date, Delaware has approximately 1.5 million active legal entities.

EXAMPLES

The following are some of the companies created in Delaware, which also have numerous subsidiaries or related entities also created in that state:

- Amazon.com
- Cirque du Soleil
- FedEx
- Google
- Hewlett-Packard
- Microsoft
- Walt Disney

PURPOSE OF A DELAWARE COMPANY

Here is a non-exhaustive list of activities that are often performed by companies created in the state of Delaware:

- Holding of interests in other companies
- Boat ownership
- Aircraft ownership
- Intellectual property ownership (e.g. trademarks, patents, copyrights, etc.)
- Services offered in several U.S. states (with employees or business places)
- Intermediary services
- Dropshipping services
- Online training courses
- Import export

In short, the state of Delaware is usually the best place in the United States to create your U.S. company.

2.4. - OTHER STATES

There may be some reasons why a person wishes to create their American company in a state other than Delaware.

BUSINESS ACTIVITY IN A SINGLE STATE

A first reason may be to carry on a commercial activity in a single state. For example, a 75-year-old man, who has always lived in New York City, wants to open a pizzeria on the corner of his street, without any idea of future expansion. In such a case, it is logical that his company should be created in the state of New York.

Let us take another example. A person wishes to purchase a property in Florida through an American company. This will be her only investment, with no idea of acquisition in a state other than Florida. Again, it makes sense that her company would be created in the state of Florida.

PROVIDE A POSITIVE PERCEPTION

A second reason may be to provide a positive perception as a result of the creation of the company in a particular state. For example, a start-up wants to fund a project via Kickstarter, a specialized crowdfunding platform. The target audience for its project is mainly located in California. In such a case, it is logical to create the new company in California.

AVOID A NEGATIVE PERCEPTION

Finally, a third reason may be to avoid a negative perception as a result of the creation of the company in a particular state. For example, a woman may want to create her company in a state other than Delaware, since that state is sometimes mistaken for a tax haven. In such a case, this lady will want to create her American company in a state that, in her opinion, attracts less attention.

However, there are significant consequences when choosing a state other than Delaware.

CREATION COSTS

First of all, let us consider the costs of creation. For example, in the state of Nevada, there are several government fees to pay when creating a company, including the costs of a Nevada Business License.

ANNUAL COSTS

We must also consider the annual costs. For example, in California, a minimum corporate tax of $800 is payable annually, regardless of sales volume.

TAX COSTS

Finally, do not forget the tax costs. Generally, if a person creates a Delaware company, but will have no physical place of business in the state, it generally does not have to pay income tax in Delaware. However, if we create a company in any other state, tax experts teach us that the income tax is payable merely because of the fact that the company was created in that state. For example, as soon as a corporation is created in the state of New York, it is required to file an income tax return in that state, regardless of the amount of its sales.

POPULAR JURISDICTIONS

Some jurisdictions are particularly popular. For example, Florida. There are a lot of economic and real estate activities in this southern state, which attracts many foreign investors. For its part, California invariably attracts web, computer, and film entrepreneurs. Finally, New York State, thanks to the city of the same name, is an incredible magnet that attracts foreign entrepreneurs from all over the world.

ONEROUS JURISDICTIONS

Take note some jurisdictions are particularly expensive, both in terms of creation costs and annual costs. These states include California, Texas, and Nevada.

Finally, here are three points you should remember.

1. FIRST POSITION

Each year, a survey is conducted among the 1,000 largest U.S. law firms. This survey includes the best place to start a company in the United States. Invariably for more than 20 years, Delaware has always finished at the top of this survey. In fact, over 95% of CorpoMax customers choose Delaware.

2. CHOICE OF JURISDICTION

You do not choose a jurisdiction to create a company like you choose a television in a big-box store. If you do not have the knowledge or training to choose the location of your American company, I strongly recommend that you seek the services of a U.S. lawyer, accountant, or tax expert.

3. BE SERIOUS!

Starting an American business is a serious operation. The search for quality information must be just as serious. In other words, be careful what you read in some blogs published by non-professionals.

3 - WHAT TYPE OF LEGAL ENTITY TO CHOOSE?

3.1 - TYPES OF LEGAL ENTITIES

The United States offers several types of legal entities through which a business can carry on activities. Among these are the following.

1. SOLE PROPRIETORSHIP

This is the simplest type of business, which you launch under your own name or under a business name.

2. PARTNERSHIP

A partnership is an agreement between two or more parties (individuals and/or businesses) to manage and operate a business and share its profits. Here are four forms of partnerships:

General Partnership

Limited Partnership

Limited Liability Partnership

Limited Liability Limited Partnership

These last three forms of partnerships are special and are often used when purchasing real estate or businesses.

3. LIMITED LIABILITY COMPANY – LLC

According to Investopedia, "A limited liability company (LLC) is a corporate structure in the United States whereby the owners are not personally liable for the company's debts or liabilities. Limited liability companies are hybrid entities that combine the characteristics of a corporation with those of a partnership or sole proprietorship."

There are mainly four forms of LLCs:

Limited Liability Company

In its basic form, this kind of LLC is the most popular in the United States.

Professional Limited Liability Company

This kind of LLC is used primarily by U.S. professionals — lawyers, accountants, architects, engineers, etc.

Public Benefit Limited Liability Company

This kind of LLC is recent in the United States and is not yet available in all states. In short, it involves a profit-oriented LLC that has a social mission intended to provide one or more benefits in the public interest and act responsibly and sustainably.

The notion of public benefit implies that the LLC must have positive effects — or reduce negative effects — for well-defined persons, entities, or communities. The types of effects include, but are not limited to the following: artistic, charitable, cultural, economic, environmental, literary, medical, religious, scientific, or technological.

It is expected that this specific kind of LLC will rarely be used.

. . .

Series LLC

Currently available in only a few states, this kind of LLC makes it possible to create an umbrella structure under which there are several sub-LLCs. This can be interesting in some areas, such as holding property or managing risky projects.

4. CORPORATIONS

According to Investopedia, "A corporation is a legal entity that is separate and distinct from its owners. Corporations enjoy most of the rights and responsibilities that individuals possess: they can enter contracts, loan and borrow money, sue and be sued, hire employees, own assets, and pay taxes."

Here are some forms of corporations:

General Corporation

It is a popular type of corporation in the United States.

We often hear the terms *C Corporation* or *S Corporation*. This is a tax distinction, not a corporate one. The tax treatment of a General Corporation is provided for in Subchapter C of the Internal Revenue Code.

However, it is possible for a General Corporation to ask the American tax authorities - Internal Revenue Service (IRS) - to cover its tax treatment under Subchapter S of the law. Without going into detail, it should simply be noted that this change in tax treatment is granted by the IRS upon request, but only if specific criteria are met. One of these criteria requires that all shareholders of the General Corporation be U.S. citizens or tax residents.

Therefore, if only one of the shareholders is not a citizen or tax resident of the United States, the General Corporation remains governed by Subchapter C of the Internal Revenue Code.

By default, a General Corporation is therefore a C Corporation.

. . .

Close Corporation

A Close Corporation, which is not very popular in the United States, is similar to a General Corporation, except in the following respects:

- First, the number of shareholders is limited to 30.
- Second, any transfer of shares must be subject to the prior approval of the directors and shareholders.
- Finally, it is forbidden to sell the shares on the public market of the stock exchange.

Professional Corporation

As in the case of the Professional LLC, the Professional Corporation is mainly used by U.S. professionals.

Non-Profit Corporation

In this case, the name says it all.

Public Benefit Corporation

A Public Benefit Corporation is similar to a Public Benefit LLC, as discussed earlier.

3.2. - CORPORATION VS. LLC

We will now focus on the two most popular types of legal entities in the United States: the General Corporation and the LLC. Let us look at their main characteristics.

Note that these are generalities only. Indeed, the corporate law of any state may contain provisions that modify or contradict these generalities. In other words, nothing can replace the wise advice of a lawyer specializing in American corporate law.

CHARACTERISTICS OF A CORPORATION

Here are the main characteristics of a corporation:

- A U.S. corporation may have an unlimited number of shareholders.
- There is no requirement for shareholders, directors, or officers of a corporation to be U.S. citizens or residents, with rare exceptions.
- The corporation has a personality distinct from its shareholders.

- A corporation offers the possibility to raise capital through the sale of shares.
- It is usually easy to transfer the shares of a corporation.
- The corporation is taxed on its own income.
- Finally, the tax rate of a corporation is generally advantageous.

CHARACTERISTICS OF AN LLC

With regard to the LLC, its main characteristics are as follows:

- The LLC may have an unlimited number of members.
- There is no obligation for members or managers of an LLC to be U.S. citizens or residents, with rare exceptions.
- The LLC has a personality distinct from its members.
- The LLC offers its members protection for their property.
- Generally, an LLC does not pay tax. The profits and losses of the LLC are allocated directly to its members, in the proportion determined by them.
- The LLC offers great flexibility in its organization.
- Finally, there may be an elimination of usual corporate formalities if this is provided for in the LLC Operating Agreement. Here, we are talking about eliminating the task of preparing minutes, holding meetings, etc. But as you know, a small pencil is often better than a large memory. As a result, American lawyers always recommend that important decisions of the LLC be documented.

STATISTICS

To give you an idea of the popularity of the corporation and the LLC, let us take a look at some statistics.

On average, more than 70% of the new entities created in Delaware are LLCs and over 20% are corporations.

For companies created through CorpoMax since 2001, 71% were LLCs and 28% were corporations.

Finally, here are three points you should remember.

1. FACTORS TO CONSIDER

Choosing the type of legal entity, either a corporation or an LLC, depends on several factors. For example, if a Canadian corporation wishes to establish a subsidiary in the United States, it generally chooses the corporation over the LLC, particularly because of the potential tax consequences. On the other hand, it is often in an individual's interest to favor the LLC over the corporation. A U.S. lawyer, accountant, or tax expert is usually the right person to advise you in this regard.

2. PUBLIC RECORDS

In Delaware, the public business register does not provide any information on the shareholders, directors, or officers of a corporation. However, corporations must file an annual report. This report contains the names and addresses of the directors and officers of the corporation. By paying the applicable government fee, anyone can get a copy of the annual reports of a corporation created in Delaware. As for LLCs, Delaware's business register also does not contain any information on an LLC's members or directors. Unlike a corporation, an LLC created in Delaware is not required to file an annual report.

3. POSSIBILITY OF CONVERSION

Generally, it is possible to convert an LLC into a corporation, or a corporation into an LLC. So if a form of legal entity has been created by mistake, it is possible to correct the situation, sometimes even in as little as half an hour.

3.3. - ARTICLES OF INCORPORATION AND BYLAWS

The articles of incorporation of a company are like its legal skeleton. The bylaws of a company are like its organs, which allow it to function. A company's articles and bylaws can be compared to the constitution and laws of a country.

ARTICLES OF A CORPORATION

As for the American corporation, its articles of incorporation may have different names, depending on the state in which it was created. We therefore generally speak of:

- Articles of Incorporation
- Certificate of Incorporation
- Corporate Charter

CONTENT OF A CORPORATION'S ARTICLES

The articles of a corporation generally contain the following elements:

1. The name of the corporation

2. The name and address of the corporation's registered agent in the state

We will see a little further what a registered agent is.

3. The nature of the corporation's activities

Often, the activities of an American corporation are described in a general way.

4. The authorized capital of the corporation

This refers to the number of shares that the corporation is entitled to issue, as well as the classes of shares, and the par value of these shares, if any. The nominal value of a share — often referred to as par value — is the value determined in the articles of incorporation.

The par value generally has no relationship with the actual value of the share. In practice, the par value is often lower than the actual value. In most cases, the articles of a corporation provide that common shares have no par value.

5. The name of the incorporator

This is the natural or legal person who prepares, signs, and submits the incorporation documents to the state. For example, CorpoMax is the incorporator of its customers' new corporations.

6. Any other provision listing the rights, powers, and obligations of the directors, officers, and shareholders of the corporation, or the limits on their rights, powers, and obligations.

BYLAWS OF A CORPORATION

For their part, the bylaws of a corporation are named:

- Bylaws — one word
- By-laws — two words separated by a hyphen

CONTENT OF A CORPORATION'S BYLAWS

The bylaws of a corporation contain a series of provisions that usually deal with the following subjects:

- The corporation's head office and place of business
- How, where, and when meetings of shareholders are to be held
- How, where, and when meetings of directors are to be held
- The shares and dividends
- The general administration of the corporation
- The corporation's books, records, and seal
- The procedure for amending the bylaws

ARTICLES OF AN LLC

As for an LLC, its articles can also have a variety of names, depending on the state in which it was created. Generally, they are referred to as:

- Articles of Organization
- Certificate of Formation
- Certificate of Organization

CONTENT OF AN LLC'S ARTICLES

The articles of an LLC generally contain the following elements:

1. The name of the LLC

2. The name and address of its registered agent in the state

3. The nature of its activities, once again described in general terms

4. The name of its organizer

This person's role is identical to that of the incorporator. A corporation is incorporated, while an LLC is organized.

5. Any other provision listing the rights, powers, and obligations of the managers and members of the LLC, or the limits on their rights, powers, and obligations.

OPERATING AGREEMENT OF AN LLC

Unlike a corporation, an LLC does not have bylaws. Instead, we refer to an operating agreement.

Again, the operating agreement can have a variety of names, depending on the state in which the LLC was created. Generally, it is referred to as:

- LLC Agreement
- Operating Agreement

CONTENT OF AN LLC AGREEMENT

The operating agreement of an LLC contains a series of provisions that usually deal with the following subjects:

- The LLC's place of business
- How, where, and when meetings of members are to be held
- How, where, and when meetings of managers are to be held
- The capital of the LLC
- The profits and losses
- The admission and withdrawal of a member
- The dissolution and winding-up of the LLC

~

Finally, here are three points you should remember.

1. CONTENT OF THE ARTICLES

U.S. lawyers recommend that the articles should not indicate the names of directors, officers, or shareholders of a corporation, or the names of directors and members of an LLC. It is preferable that this information, which is subject to change over time, should instead be recorded in the company's minutes. This approach also ensures greater discretion.

2. NATURE OF THE ACTIVITIES

The exact nature of the activities of a corporation or an LLC is almost never specified in the articles. At most, there is a general description, which gives the company a great deal of latitude.

3. LANGUAGE OF THE OPERATING AGREEMENT

In general, the operating agreement of an LLC can be written in any language. It can even be verbal. In the latter case, U.S. lawyers raise the fact that a verbal operating agreement may pose significant evidentiary problems if a dispute arises between the parties involved.

3.4 - BUSINESS PURPOSE

The business purpose of a company is the nature of the activities that this company can carry out.

In Europe, a business can usually carry on the activities specifically listed in its articles of incorporation. In the United States, the situation is completely opposite. An American company can carry out any legal activity. It is therefore not required to specify the exact nature of its activities in its corporate charter.

The articles of incorporation of a U.S. corporation generally include the following provision:

"The purpose of the Corporation is to engage in any lawful act or activity for which corporations may be organized under the law..."

A similar provision is found in the certificate of formation of an LLC.

Therefore, a U.S. company can do everything, except what is:

- Illegal — for example, selling cocaine
- Regulated — for example, operating a bank or insurance company

In the latter case, the company must obtain the necessary authorizations from the appropriate government agencies.

ACTIVITIES

This means that a U.S. company can carry out many different activities. For example, Apple sells both computers and phones as well as cloud services.

Sometimes it is better to create one company per type of activity. For example, Amazon sells consumer products while one of its subsidiaries, Amazon Web Services, sells cloud services.

Finally, in some cases, it is preferable to create several companies that carry out the same activity. For example, Cirque du Soleil creates a specific company for each of its shows. This allows it to divide the risks associated with its sometimes dangerous activities.

NAICS

Even if a company is not required to specify the nature of its activities in its articles, there is still a system for classifying the business activities of a U.S. company.

This system is called NAICS, which stands for *North American Industry Classification System*. The NAICS code consists of five or six digits. It is used in the United States, Canada, and Mexico.

Some U.S. states require companies doing business on their territory to specify the nature of their activities. These companies must therefore provide the NAICS code related to their activities. However, it should be noted that this is by no means restrictive. This does not preclude companies from engaging in activities other than those related to the NAICS code of their core business. Also, in the context of certain government tenders, interested companies must provide the NAICS code related to the activities covered by the call for tenders.

D-U-N-S

There is another well-known number in the United States, the D-U-N-S number. D-U-N-S stands for *Data Universal Numbering System.* It consists of a nine-digit number issued by the U.S. firm Dun & Bradstreet. The D-U-N-S number identifies a specific company. Dun & Bradstreet establishes a complete record on this company, especially at the financial level.

There is no cost for obtaining a D-U-N-S number. Sometimes, it can take up to 30 days until the number is attributed.

The D-U-N-S number is required by some U.S. government agencies, especially if your company supplies goods or services to the U.S. government.

3.5 - CAPITAL STOCK

In the United States, a corporation's capital is referred to as:

- Capital Stock
- Share Capital

It represents the value of the investment in the capital of the corporation. What is interesting is that there is no mandatory minimum capital. So the sum of $1 can be the starting capital. On the other hand, unlike what is done in Europe, the amount of the capital stock is never mentioned in the description of the company.

SHARES OF A CORPORATION

Regarding the type of shares of a corporation, there are mainly two.

On the one hand, there are common shares. These shares almost always give the right to vote. They are often called control shares. In particular, they allow the election of directors.

On the other hand, there are preferred shares. These generally do not give the right to vote. However, they are entitled to a preferred dividend that is usually payable before any dividend can be declared on the common shares.

Also, please note that there may be several classes of preferred shares, with specific rights for each.

AUTHORIZED CAPITAL VS. ISSUED CAPITAL

Finally, we must distinguish between the authorized capital and the issued capital. The authorized capital stock is the number of shares that the corporation has the right to issue, which is indicated in its articles. The issued capital stock is the number of shares that the corporation has actually issued to shareholders.

For example, XYZ Inc. has an authorized capital stock of 1,500 common shares. Then, the company issues 100 shares in your favor. This represents the issued capital stock. This leaves 1,400 common shares available for future issuance.

CAPITAL OF AN LLC

As for the LLC, its capital has various names:

- LLC Capital
- Member Capital
- Membership Capital

Again, the term refers to the initial investment in the LLC's capital. As with a corporation, the minimum required capital is usually just $1.

UNITS OF AN LLC

In the case of an LLC, we refer to units rather than shares. There are a variety of names:

- LLC Units
- LLC Interest
- Membership Units
- Membership Interest

Unlike a corporation, an LLC does not have an authorized capital. Therefore, an LLC can usually issue as many units as it wants.

Finally, here are three points you should remember.

1. PROFESSIONALS

In some situations, it may be beneficial to consult a U.S. lawyer, accountant, or tax expert before establishing the authorized capital stock of your corporation. For example, say you want to create a class of shares to attract potential investors. In such a case, a qualified professional will be able to assist you.

2. KEY EMPLOYEES

Perhaps your corporation has key employees whose services it wants to retain for many years. In this case, it may be advisable for the capital stock of your corporation to have a class of shares designed specifically to attract this type of employee. Once again, a qualified professional can assist you for that purpose.

3. LIMITED AUTHORIZED CAPITAL STOCK

In the case of a corporation, it is often preferable to limit the authorized capital stock. An overly high authorized capital stock can have a negative impact on the amount of the annual franchise tax, as we will see later on.

3.6 - SHAREHOLDERS

In the case of a corporation, the holders of shares are referred to as:

- Shareholders
- Stockholders

A shareholder is a person who holds all or part of the shares issued by the corporation.

- A shareholder who holds 100% of the issued shares is called the *Sole Shareholder*.
- A shareholder who holds more than 50% and less than 100% of the issued shares is called the *Majority Shareholder*.
- A shareholder who holds less than 50% of the issued shares is called a *Minority Shareholder*.
- Two shareholders who each hold 50% of the issued shares are called *Equal Shareholders*.

WHO CAN BE A SHAREHOLDER?

The shareholder of a corporation may be a natural person or a legal entity. So, a company can be a shareholder of a corporation.

There is no requirement for U.S. citizenship or residence for shareholders of a corporation, except in certain cases, including the following:

- National security — for example, in a sensitive area, such as weapons manufacturing
- Aircraft ownership
- S corporations

MEMBER

In the case of a Limited Liability Company, we are not talking about shareholders but rather members.

A member is a person who holds all or part of the units issued by the LLC.

Again, the member may be a natural person or a legal entity.

Finally, as in the case of a corporation, it is not mandatory for a member of an LLC to be a U.S. citizen or resident, except in certain cases, including the following:

- National security
- Aircraft ownership

~

Finally, here are three points you should remember.

1. NUMBER OF SHAREHOLDERS

Even though a U.S. company may have an unlimited number of shareholders or members, it is sometimes preferable to limit the number. In the case of a small business, it is often complicated to manage a large number of shareholders, especially when some of them leave or die.

2. PERCENTAGE

Majority shareholder, minority shareholder, or equal shareholder — what to choose? There is no ideal percentage. It all depends on the relationship between the people involved. But in practice, when only two people are involved, it is preferable that each person owns 50% of the issued shares. When there are several shareholders, it is normal that some of them may be in the minority.

Based on nearly 40 years of experience with entrepreneurs, I can tell you that companies that last the longest are those with a single shareholder or two equal shareholders.

3. ACTIVE VS. PASSIVE

When there are active and passive shareholders, this sometimes leads to disputes over the management of the company, and therefore to potential litigation. In short, before you become a shareholder of a company, take the time to get to know the people who will be shareholders with you.

3.7 - DIRECTORS AND OFFICERS

An American corporation is administered by directors. Generally, directors must be natural persons. Consequently, a corporation cannot act as a director of another corporation. Directors are elected by the shareholders, normally in proportion to the shares held by each of them. There are no U.S. citizenship or residency requirements for corporate directors, with rare exceptions.

OFFICERS OF A CORPORATION

The officers of a corporation are appointed by the directors.

The titles of officers are normally as follows:

- President
- Vice President
- Secretary
- Treasurer

As a general rule, the officers of a corporation must be natural persons. They can be chosen from among the directors, but this is not mandatory.

It is also not mandatory that all officer titles be held. For example, a corporation may have only a president, or a president and a secretary. On the other hand, the same person may wear several hats as an officer. For example, a person may be the president, secretary, and treasurer of a corporation. As with directors, there are no U.S. citizenship or residency requirements for officers, with rare exceptions.

MANAGERS OF AN LLC

For its part, the LLC is managed by managers.

The titles of the managers of an LLC are generally as follows:

- Operating Manager
- Vice Operating Manager
- Secretary Manager
- Treasurer Manager

Unlike a corporation, a legal entity can generally be an LLC manager. For example, an American or foreign company may be the manager of an LLC. But in practice, it is quite rare. Again, there is no requirement for U.S. citizenship or residency for managers of an LLC, with rare exceptions.

Finally, here are three points you should remember.

1. NUMBER OF DIRECTORS

It is generally recommended to limit the number of directors. Ideally, their number should not exceed four. The more numerous the directors, the more complicated and cumbersome the administration of the company will be.

2. MAJORITY SHAREHOLDER

When one shareholder owns 90% of the issued shares and the other shareholder owns 10%, should the corporation have two directors? Normally, the answer is no. When there is a majority shareholder of such importance, they usually are the only director and, therefore, the only authorized signatory to the bank.

3. MANAGEMENT BY THE MEMBERS

It is permissible for an LLC to be managed by its own members, rather than by managers. It is therefore not mandatory to appoint managers. In such a case, this LLC is described as a Member-Managed LLC. However, in practice, it is not recommended. It is useful for an LLC to be run by managers, especially in relation to third parties. Customers, employees, suppliers, and bankers expect LLC representatives to have an official title.

3.8 - CORPORATE LEDGER AND SEAL

Following the creation of your American company, the legal documents concerning it are normally inserted in a corporate ledger.

This workbook contains tabs that clearly identify the nature of the documents that are part of it.

TAB 1

Under the first tab of the binder, there are the official certificates issued by the state, whether or not supported by an apostille:

- Certificate of incorporation or formation
- Certificate of good standing
- Certificate of incumbency

Previously, we have seen what the certificate of incorporation or formation consists of.

But what about the other two certificates?

. . .

Certificate of Good Standing

The Certificate of Good Standing is an official document issued by the state, which generally confirms the following elements:

- The creation of the company
- The date of its creation
- The existence of the company on the date of issue of the certificate
- The filing of all annual reports required by the state
- The payment of all corporate taxes payable to the state

Certificate of Incumbency

The Certificate of Incumbency is a document that generally certifies the following elements:

- The name of the company
- The date of its creation
- The legal form of the company — for example, a corporation or an LLC
- The place where the company was created — for example, the state of Delaware
- The company's registration number on the state register
- The name of the shareholders or members of the company
- The number of shares or units held by each shareholder or member
- The percentage of shares or units held by each shareholder or member
- The name of the directors or managers
- The names and titles of the officers — for example, president, vice president, secretary, and treasurer
- The name of the company's registered agent in the state
- The address of the company's registered office in the state

The Certificate of Incumbency is often prepared and signed by the incorporator or organizer before a commissioner for oaths - called a *Notary Public* in the United States.

This certificate is often useful to confirm to third parties the power of directors and officers as authorized representatives of the company.

For example, in Delaware, there is no other way to confirm such power. Indeed, the state's commercial register is silent on the identity of the directors, officers, and shareholders of the companies created there. However, in the case of corporations, it is possible to obtain a copy of the corporate report, which must be filed on an annual basis. In the case of LLCs, there is no requirement to file a corporate report.

Apostille

An apostille is an official document of the state, accompanied by a special seal, that certifies one or the other of the following facts:

- A document is a true copy of the original.
- A document was signed before a state's notary public.

The apostille therefore gives the document a character of authenticity, which is then recognized almost everywhere in the world.

TAB 2

Under the second tab of the binder are the bylaws of the corporation or the operating agreement of the LLC.

TAB 3

Under the third tab are the minutes and resolutions adopted by the incorporators, directors, officers, and shareholders of the corporation, or by the organizers, managers, and members of the LLC.

TAB 4

Under the fourth tab are the share certificates or unit certificates.

TAB 5

Under the fifth tab is the register of shareholders or members, including the following information for each of them:

- Name
- Address
- Telephone number
- E-mail address
- Nature and number of shares or units held

TAB 6

Finally, under the sixth tab is the register of share or unit transfers.

CERTIFICATE OF SHARES OF A CORPORATION

Now, let us look at what a corporation's share certificate is.

At the top of the certificate, we usually see the elements specific to the corporation:

- The name of the corporation
- The jurisdiction under which the corporation was created – for example, Delaware
- The amount of the authorized capital stock
- The par value attributed to the shares – if there is such a value
- The class of shares – common or preferred

Then, there are the elements specific to the certificate issued in favor of the shareholder of the corporation:

1. The certificate number — usually at the top left

The first certificate issued by the corporation is numbered 1. If there is a second shareholder, the certificate representing their shares will be number 2.

If the authorized capital stock of the corporation includes more than one class of shares — for example, Class A, B, and C shares —, the numbering of the certificates may include the letter of the class involved and the certificate number. For example, the first Class A share certificate will be numbered A-1, followed by A-2, A-3, etc. The same logic will apply to Class B and C share certificates.

2. The number of shares issued — usually at the top right of the certificate

3. The name of the shareholder who holds the shares

4. The number of shares issued, this time in letters and numerals

5. The date of issue of the certificate, in U.S. format — i.e., month, day and year

6. The names and titles of the officers who sign the certificate — often the president and secretary

In the United States, a signature must be affixed on the line provided for this purpose. If the signature is affixed elsewhere than on the line, the document is generally presumed unsigned.

TRANSFER OF SHARES OF A CORPORATION

In the event of a transfer of shares of a corporation, the back of the certificate must be completed.

. . .

Here are the elements that it should generally include:

1. The name of the transferee of the shares - therefore, the name of the person to whom the shares are transferred

2. The number of shares transferred

If the owner of these shares wants to transfer all of them, they indicate the total number of shares specified on the front of the certificate, generally in letters and numerals.

But if the owner wants to transfer only part of the shares, they then indicate the number of shares transferred. In the latter case, the transferor shareholder's share certificate is then cancelled and replaced by two new share certificates:

- The first certificate - representing the shares transferred - is issued in the name of the new shareholder.
- The second certificate - representing the shares held - is issued in the name of the transferring shareholder.

3. The name of the lawyer who is registering the transfer

If no lawyer is involved in the case, simply indicate N/A for *Not Applicable*.

4. The date of the transfer of shares, in U.S. format

5. The name of the transferring shareholder who signs on the line provided

6. The name of the witness, who also signs on the line provided

Note that the presence of a witness, without being mandatory, is recommended. In addition, nothing prevents the new shareholder from signing as a witness to the signature of the transferring shareholder.

CERTIFICATE OF UNITS OF AN LLC

With regard to the unit certificate of an LLC, the first elements are:

- The name of the LLC
- The jurisdiction under which the LLC was created

It should be noted that the LLC can normally issue an unlimited number of units, which generally have no nominal value. Now, let us look at the specific elements of the certificate issued in favor of the LLC member:

1. The certificate number

2. The number of units represented by the certificate

3. The name of the member who holds the units

4. The number of units issued, in letters and numerals

5. The date of issue of the certificate

6. The names and titles of the managers who sign — often the Operating Manager and the Secretary Manager

TRANSFER OF UNITS OF AN LLC

In the event of a transfer of units of an LLC, the back of the certificate must be completed.

Here are the elements it must include:

1. The name of the member acquiring the units

2. The number of units transferred, in letters and numerals

3. The name of the lawyer recording the transfer, if applicable

4. The date of transfer of units

5. The name of the transferor, who signs

6. The name of the witness, who also signs

COLOR OF CERTIFICATES AND SEAL

In the case of a corporation, when there are several classes of shares involved, the share certificates generally have a different color per class, which greatly facilitates their identification.

Finally, an American binder often contains a corporate seal, which some call a dry stamp. The imprint of this seal may be affixed in particular to the certificates of shares or units, as well as to certain important documents.

Finally, here are three points you should remember.

1. MANDATORY?

Is it mandatory for a corporation or an LLC to have a corporate ledger? Generally no. But it is strongly recommended to have one. This makes it much easier to keep the corporate and official documents of the American company, in the same place and in an orderly manner.

2. CORPORATE SEAL

In the United States, the use of the corporate seal is much less widespread than in Europe. For Americans, it is a vestige of the past, to which some are still attached.

3. CERTIFICATES

Original share or unit certificates are often kept in the corporate ledger. However, a copy of these documents shall be given to each of their holders. This makes it easier to find the original certificates, especially when there is a transfer or cancellation of shares or units.

4 - REGISTERED AGENT OF YOUR COMPANY

4.1. - WHAT IS A REGISTERED AGENT?

A registered agent is a natural or legal person who resides in the state where your American company was created or in the state where your company does business. For example, your company was incorporated in the State of Delaware and obtained authorization to do business in Florida. You will therefore need to hire a registered agent in both states.

AVAILABILITY OF THE REGISTERED AGENT

The registered agent must normally be available:

- At home or office, as the case may be
- From 9 a.m. to 5 p.m.
- Monday to Friday
- 52 weeks a year

ROLE OF THE REGISTERED AGENT

The role of the registered agent is twofold:

- First, the registered agent represents your company for the purpose of receiving any documents of a legal nature. For example, a judicial document means a formal notice, a legal procedure, or a notice of sale for unpaid taxes.
- Second, the registered agent usually receives, on behalf of your company, the annual corporate tax notices and the annual report notices sent by the State.

Finally, here are three points you should remember.

1. LEGAL DOCUMENTS

For litigators, the eighth wonder of the world is the registered agent of a company they are mandated to prosecute. They do not have to ask themselves where court documents should be served. Is it at the company's head office? Or at one of its places of business? No. They simply have to serve the court documents on the registered agent of the company being prosecuted. As soon as the registered agent is served with the judicial document, the time limits for responding to the judicial petition, or appearing before the court, normally begin to run.

2. COMMERCIAL AGENTS

In the United States, registered agents are usually legal persons. CorpoMax is one of the commercial registered agents in the State of Delaware. Since 2001, CorpoMax has acted as registered agent for thousands of companies created in this state. CorpoMax also provides a full range of registered agent services in the other 49 U.S. states, using its national network of commercial agents.

The advantage of dealing with a commercial registered agent is obvious. This agent meets the availability obligation required by law, which is to be available from 9 a.m. to 5 p.m., Monday to Friday, 52 weeks a year.

3. RESPONSIBILITY

Upon service of a judicial document, the registered agent must, without delay, forward the document to the company they represent. Indeed, the time limits for responding or appearing in court generally begin to run as soon as the registered agent receives the judicial document. These deadlines are sometimes very short. Therefore, the registered agent has an important legal responsibility.

4.2 - HOW TO CHOOSE YOUR REGISTERED AGENT

In most cases, the corporate service provider that creates your corporation or LLC will also act as its registered agent.

COST OF SERVICES

The choice of your registered agent is partly based on the annual price of its services. Some corporate service providers charge a relatively low price for the creation of your company, but charge an exorbitant annual fee to act as a registered agent. It is like buying a car. You have to consider not only the purchase price, but also the cost of maintenance.

Here are the people to avoid, which you should never use to act as a registered agent for your U.S. company.

FAMILY MEMBER

The first person to avoid is a member of your family - immediate or distant. It is not their mission to act as a registered agent for your company. Often without knowing it, they bear a huge legal responsibility. In addition, they will obviously never be able to comply with the availability rule imposed by the state, that is, to be available at their home or office, from 9 a.m. to 5 p.m., Monday to Friday, 52 weeks a year.

FRIEND

The second person to avoid is a friend. It is not because your friend resides in the state of your company that it will make them an effective registered agent. In addition, they will not be able to respect the rule of availability imposed by the state. So, if you want to keep your friends, do not retain their services as a registered agent.

EMPLOYEE

The third person to avoid is an employee. Retaining the services of an employee to act as the registered agent of your company is a serious mistake. Your employee may forget to hand over a legal document they have received, or may quite simply misplace it. In addition, there is always the possibility that, one day, your company and your employee will have opposing interests, especially if you have a falling out. An employee is really not a good choice as a registered agent for your American company.

BUSINESS PARTNER

The fourth person to avoid is a business partner. Here, this expression is understood in its broadest sense. This includes a customer, subcontractor, or supplier. For the same reasons as those stated for the employee, it is absolutely not recommended to use the services of a business partner to act as a registered agent of your company.

YOURSELF

The last person to avoid is yourself. Some entrepreneurs wish to act as a registered agent for their company. Do not make this mistake! It is obvious that you will not comply with the availability obligation discussed earlier. This is even more true if you do not reside in the state or if you only have a secondary residence there.

Finally, here are three points you should remember.

1. EQUALITY?

Not all registered agents are equal. For example, with regard to the annual tax notice sent by the state, some agents simply send it by regular mail to their customers, without any follow-up. However, penalties are often very significant in the event of non-payment of the annual tax within the prescribed time limit. For example, in the State of Delaware, the automatic penalty for failure to file or late filing of the annual report is $200, while in Florida, the penalty is $400. Fortunately, other registered agents, few in number but highly professional, send an email to their customers, followed by one or two reminders in the event of non-payment of the tax before the deadline expires.

In the State of Delaware, some registered agents have direct access to the Corporations Division's computer system. These are called *Registered Agents with Remote Access*. This can be a very important advantage for you in terms of speed. For example, you need a Certificate of Good Standing without delay. An ordinary registered agent can obtain it within 24 hours. A registered agent with remote access can obtain it in just a few minutes. CorpoMax is one of the registered agents with remote access in the State of Delaware.

2. COMMUNICATION

It is important to consider the ease of communication with the registered agent of your U.S. company. Will you be able to contact your agent by phone, or will you spend your time exchanging with a voicemail? Will your agent reply to your email the same day or two weeks later? Will your agent speak your language or will you have to search for your words while trying to speak their own?

3. ONE-STOP SHOP

If your company was created in Delaware and does business in California and Florida, then it needs a registered agent in all three states. It may be convenient to retain the services of a registered agent who has a network of agents throughout the United States. It is thus a one-stop shop for you, which facilitates communication and simplifies invoicing.

5 - DOMICILIATION OF YOUR COMPANY

5.1 - IMPORTANCE OF AN ADDRESS IN THE UNITED STATES

It is important, and above all logical, that your American company has an address in the United States. Just as a French company must have an address in France, and a Canadian company must have an address in Canada.

So, remember that an American company with no U.S. address is a situation to avoid. Also note that the address of your registered agent is not the address of your company in the United States, unless this agent also offers a domiciliation service.

POTENTIAL CUSTOMERS

The importance of an address on U.S. soil is easily verified in the eyes of potential customers of your company. They will want to do business with a U.S. company that has a U.S. address. In addition, many American customers will want to pay by check or domestic bank transfer only. They will refuse to make international bank transfers, especially because of conversion fees and bank charges.

. . .

Always remember the following logic:

- A U.S. company
- A U.S. address
- A U.S. bank account
- A U.S. phone number

If any element is missing, the logic will not be respected and your potential customers will ask questions.

SUPPLIERS

The reasoning is similar with regard to suppliers of your company. First, a significant number of U.S. suppliers only deliver their products within the United States. It is therefore important that you choose an address that accepts such deliveries. Moreover, the reasoning also applies to U.S. banks. They have several requirements, including the address of your company, which must be located in the United States.

Now, for postal purposes, let us talk about the format of a physical address on U.S. soil.

For example, take the following address:

HELLO LLC
123 MAIN STREET
STE 200
NEWARK, DE 19711

NAME OF THE RECIPIENT

First of all, you have to indicate the name of the recipient. There is a significant difference between the U.S. postal system and, for example, the French one. In France, the postman does not deliver to an address, but rather to a person. If he does not know the recipient of the shipment, or if the recipient's name is not affixed to the mailbox, the French postman does not usually deliver the envelope. In the United States, the postman does not deliver to a person, but rather to an address. So we can indicate *Santa Claus* or *Mr. Nobody* on the envelope, and the mail will still be delivered.

CIVIC ADDRESS

Then, you have to indicate the building number, followed by the street name. If there is an office or apartment number, it appears after the street or on the line below. There are several ways to identify any internal unit, including the following:

STE : Short version of *Suite*

APT : Short version of *Apartment*

 # : Pound sign, also called *hashtag* or *pound symbol*

CITY, STATE, AND ZIP CODE

On the next line is the name of the city, followed by the state acronym — two letters — and the postal code, which is called the *zip code* in the United States. It is very important to indicate the name or acronym of the state after the city. For example, there are at least ten states in the U.S. with a city called *Newark.*

On the other hand, the zip code has two versions:

Short Version: consisting of five digits, which is most commonly used

Long Version: consisting of nine digits, which further specifies the location of the building

P.O. BOX

If your recipient has a post office box in the United States (called *P.O. Box)*, the format of the address is slightly different. For example, let us take the following address:

MR. JOHN SMITH
P.O. BOX 300
NEWARK, DE 19714

On the first line is the name of the recipient. If this name is not registered with the post office that houses the mailbox, the shipment will usually be returned to the sender. However, it is possible to add more than one name to the register for the same P.O. box.

On the second line is the P.O. box number.

On the third line are the city, state, and zip code.

In any case, when the letter or package comes from abroad, it is obviously necessary to indicate the country, that is to say *United States*, *United States of America*, or the initials *USA*.

5.2 - ADDRESS IN THE UNITED STATES: WHERE?

When your new American company begins its operations, it will not necessarily have a physical place of business. It will probably use a virtual address, which is also referred to as domiciliation. This will allow you to discover your new environment quietly, at a low cost, and to analyze the business opportunities available to you. In addition, some companies simply do not need a physical address. We can think of all those who work exclusively on the Internet.

Now let us see where your new American company can establish its domiciliation.

REGISTERED AGENT

The first solution is to use the address of your registered agent, if it offers professional domiciliation services. There are few registered agents offering such a service in the United States.

Indeed, the service of domiciliation requires a regular and efficient forwarding of mail and parcels that your company can receive. Not all registered agents can provide reliable service in this regard.

SHAREHOLDER

Another solution is to use the address of one of your company's shareholders, who lives in the United States.

Generally, it will be an active and reliable shareholder, holding at least 50% of the shares. However, will this shareholder want their residential address to become public?

DIRECTOR OR OFFICER

A third solution is to use the address of one of your company's directors or officers. Again, the same arguments regarding residential address apply.

RENTAL AGENCY

Finally, another solution is to use the services of an agency specializing in temporary rental of commercial space.

This solution can be interesting if you need to use an office space on a temporary or intermittent basis, for example to meet a customer. However, the costs of such an agency are generally quite high.

After discussing acceptable domiciliation addresses, let us now look at which ones to avoid.

FAMILY MEMBER

First, it is recommended that you never use the address of a family member who resides in the United States. Despite close family ties, situations may arise that will prevent this person from forwarding the mail or parcels to you effectively. Again, will this family member want to see their residential address listed on your company's website?

FRIEND

Similar reasoning applies if you plan to use a friend's address. They will certainly agree to provide you with a service on an *ad hoc* basis, but not necessarily on an ongoing basis.

EMPLOYEE

Another address to avoid is that of an employee of your company. As in the case of a marriage, the initial relationship is generally positive. However, if your interests eventually diverge, it will be problematic if your company's address is established at your former employee's home.

BUSINESS PARTNER

It is also not recommended to establish the address of your U.S. company with a business partner, whether a customer, subcontractor, or supplier.

First of all, your interests may eventually diverge over time. Then, they are already busy with running their own business. Imagine if, in addition, they must take care of managing your mail and parcels.

YOURSELF

Finally, if you are thinking of using your own residential address in the United States, consider that it is not necessarily a good idea. Do you really want your home address to be known to everyone, for example, a customer or supplier with whom you may have difficulty one day?

Finally, here are three points you should remember.

1. TAXATION

Some U.S. states are very aggressive in tax matters. These include California, New Jersey, Texas, and New York State. You must therefore be aware of the tax consequences that may arise from the establishment of a domiciliation in any of these states. The simple fact of indicating a domiciliation address on your company's website may potentially be of interest to the state concerned.

2. RENTAL AGENCY

If you decide to enter into a domiciliation agreement with a rental agency, it is strongly recommended that you read the agreement carefully before signing it. It often happens that some agencies charge significant fees, penalties, and interest in a variety of situations that may arise. Among these, one can think of a breach of the contract before its expiry.

3. IMPORTANT CHOICE

The decision you are going to make regarding the domiciliation of your company is of great importance. You must ensure that communication with the person or company providing the domiciliation service will be easy and efficient. The redirection of mail and parcels must be carried out on a regular basis. This is crucial, especially with regard to correspondence from the IRS, which is the U.S. tax body. In some situations, if you do not respond to a letter from the IRS within the prescribed time, an automatic fine of $10,000 may be imposed on your company. Now you probably have a better understanding of the importance of the choice you are going to make.

5.3 - TELEPHONE NUMBER

A U.S. phone number consists of 10 digits.

In writing, we see (302) 266-8200, 302-266-8200 or 302 266 8200.

Orally, we say 3-0-2 (pause) 2-6-6 (pause) 8-2-0-0, pronouncing each digit individually.

If a call is made from abroad to the United States, this number must be preceded by the U.S. country code, which is 1. For example, if a call is made from France, you have to dial 00 to leave France, 1 for the United States and finally 302 266 8200.

AREA CODE

The first three digits of the telephone number represent the area code. For example, in Delaware, there is only one area code, which is 302. Twelve U.S. states have only one area code.

However, the most populous states have several area codes:

- California: 32
- Texas: 27
- Florida: 19
- New York State: 18

MOBILE PHONE NUMBERS

U.S. mobile phone numbers do not have any particular identification, unlike French mobile numbers, which start with 06 or 07.

TOLL-FREE NUMBERS

There are also toll-free numbers. These numbers are very popular with Americans and give a professional image to the companies that own them. The area code for this type of number is generally 800, 833, 844, 855, 866, 877 or 888.

Without a doubt, the best-known toll-free number in the United States is that of FedEx. It is easy to remember, because it is made up mainly of letters: 1-800-GO-FEDEX. The caller must therefore convert the letters to numbers using the phone keypad. In fact, this is what has reduced the popularity of these types of numbers in the United States.

When a phone call is made from the United States to a toll-free number, the caller does not pay any long-distance charges. However, these toll-free numbers are rarely accessible from abroad.

VIRTUAL PHONE NUMBERS

When you start your business in the United States, you can easily get a virtual phone number. It is recommended to choose this type of number according to the address of your company. For example, if the address is located in the state of Delaware, the telephone number should begin with 302.

. . .

When you set up your company's virtual phone number, you can usually record your own greeting. This message can be bilingual - English and French, English and Spanish, etc. - or simply in English, depending on your target clientele. Of course, do not settle for the default greeting, usually provided by the telephone company.

Finally, many will set up automatic call forwarding, particularly to their mobile phone.

MOBILE PHONE PROVIDERS

In the United States, the main providers of mobile phone numbers are:

- AT&T
- Cellular One
- Google Fi
- T-Mobile
- U.S. Cellular
- Verizon Wireless
- Virgin Mobile

You can usually get a SIM card or phone with a SIM card from these companies. Prepaid accounts are also available. However, it is important to note that an American address is usually required to obtain a U.S. mobile phone.

TELECOPIER - FAX

Telecopiers, commonly known as *fax*, are still widely used in the United States. The U.S. tax authority, the IRS, as well as some states, suppliers, and customers use it on a daily basis. Many see this as an advantage, particularly in terms of the security of exchanges. Often, when you get a virtual phone number, it also allows you to receive faxes.

. . .

Finally, here are three points you should remember.

1. U.S. TELEPHONE NUMBER

If you are starting your business in the United States, it is crucial to have a U.S. phone number. Never forget that Americans buy first and foremost American. To do this, you must make it easier for them to communicate with your company.

2. BENEFITS OF A MOBILE PHONE

There are several advantages to having an American mobile phone. It can be useful when you travel to the United States. Most importantly, it allows you to easily receive text or SMS messages sent by your bank for security or validation purposes.

3. TEXT MESSAGES OR SMS

Some virtual phone number providers also offer the option of receiving text messages or SMS. However, these web-based solutions are rarely as effective as a real American mobile phone. On the other hand, U.S. SIM cards can usually be purchased online.

6 - ANNUAL CORPORATE OBLIGATIONS

6.1 - ANNUAL REPORT

The annual report of your American company is a corporate form that you normally have to complete once a year, directly on the state's website. This report contains various information, such as:

- The name of the company
- The address of the company
- The name and mailing address of the directors or managers
- The name, title, and mailing address of the officers.

However, the name and address of the shareholders of a corporation or members of an LLC are almost never required.

DESIGNATIONS

The name of the annual report varies by state and type of entity. Here are some names:

- Annual Certificate
- Annual Franchise Tax Report
- Annual List of Managers or Members - LLC
- Annual List of Officers - corporations
- Annual Registration Report
- Annual Renewal Report
- Annual Report
- Biennial Occupation Tax Report
- Biennial Report
- Biennial Statement
- Business Entity Report
- Decennial Report
- Periodic Report
- Public Information Report
- Statement of Information
- Two-Year Report

OBLIGATION TO FILE

The obligation to file an annual report varies according to the nature of the legal entities and the states. For example, in Delaware and Arizona, the obligation to file an annual report is imposed only on corporations. In Oklahoma, the opposite is true: only LLCs must file this report. In Alabama, there is no requirement for corporations or LLCs to file an annual report. However, some corporate information is required in their tax return.

FILING FREQUENCY

The filing frequency of the annual report varies according to the nature of the legal entities and the states:

- In some states, the annual report must be filed no later than the company's anniversary date. For a domestic company —

created in the state —, the anniversary date is the date of its creation. For a foreign company — created in another state —, the anniversary date is the date of its registration in the state's corporate register. For example, your company was created on January 8, 2020. Therefore, you must file its annual report no later than January 8, 2021.

- In other states, the annual report must be filed no later than the end of the month of the company's anniversary date. For example, your company was created on March 14, 2020. You will therefore have to file its annual report no later than March 31, 2021.
- In other states, the annual report must be filed no later than the last day of the month preceding the company's anniversary date. For example, your company was created on February 7, 2020. You will therefore have to file its annual report no later than January 31, 2021.
- In other states, this filing takes place at the latest on a fixed date. For example, in Delaware, the annual corporation report must be filed by March 1 of every year.
- In other states, the annual report is required within a fixed period of time following the end of the company's financial year. For example, your company has a December 31 year-end. If the law requires the annual report within three months of the end of that fiscal year, the annual report must be filed no later than March 31 of the following year.
- In other states, the annual report must be filed within the quarter relating to the company's anniversary date. For example, your company was created on January 15, 2020. You will therefore have to file its annual report between January 1 and March 31, 2021.
- Finally, in other states, the corporate report must be filed not on an annual basis, but rather every two years. For example, your company was created on January 15, 2020 in New York State. You will therefore have to file its first Biennial

Statement no later than January 31, 2022. In Pennsylvania, the corporate report must be filed every 10 years.

FAILURE TO FILE THE ANNUAL REPORT

If your U.S. company fails to file its annual report within the statutory deadline, it automatically ceases to be in compliance - *Good Standing*. This prevents it from initiating legal proceedings or bidding on public projects.

If your company fails to file its annual report for two years in the state where it was created, it is automatically dissolved in most states.

If your company fails to file its annual report for two years in the state where it obtained the authorization to do business, its entry on the company register is automatically deleted in most states.

It is generally possible to revive the dissolved company or the registration of the foreign company by filing all missing annual reports and paying government fees as well as interest and penalties.

Finally, here are three points you should remember.

1. CONFUSION

Do not confuse the annual report with the tax return of the company. The annual report is only a corporate report, and generally has no relationship to the company's revenues.

2. CONFIDENTIALITY

In the annual report, it is recommended that the address of your company be indicated as the correspondence address for each director and officer. In general, you should avoid giving the residential addresses of the directors and officers of your U.S. company, since the information provided in the annual report is normally publicly available.

3. EIN NUMBER

Some states require that you indicate the EIN - Employer Identification Number - of your company in its annual report. Many of these states allow easy access to annual reports and even display the companies' EIN on their website. This poses a clear risk of corporate identity theft.

6.2 - CORPORATE TAX

In addition to the annual report, your U.S. company must generally pay a corporate tax to the state in which it was created or to the state where it obtained authorization to do business.

NAME

The name of this tax varies by state and by nature of legal entities. In the case of corporations, the tax is usually referred to as a *Franchise Tax*. In the case of LLCs, it is simply referred to as the *LLC Tax*.

AMOUNT

Again, the amount of tax varies from state to state and from legal entity to legal entity.

In some states, the amount of the tax is a flat rate.

In other states, the amount of tax varies. For example, in Delaware, the amount of corporate tax payable by a corporation varies between $225 and $200,000, depending on the amount of authorized capital.

Regarding the LLC tax, Delaware is claiming a flat rate of $300.

In some states, there is no corporate tax to pay.

PENALTY

If the corporate tax is not paid within the prescribed period, there is usually a penalty to pay. In some states, this penalty is minimal. In other states, such as Florida, the penalty is $400.

6.3 - FEES OF THE REGISTERED AGENT

In addition to the annual corporate tax, your U.S. company must pay the fees of its registered agent.

These fees typically range from $50 to $500 a year.

At $50, you can easily guess that the level of service provided by the registered agent will be minimal.

At $500, the price is certainly too high.

A reasonable average is between $125 and $175 a year.

But please, do not choose the registered agent of your company solely on the basis of the annual price of its services.

Take the time to analyze the nature and extent of the services your agent will provide to your company, as well as the ease of communication.

7 - EIN NUMBER AND TAXATION

7.1 - EIN NUMBER

The EIN, an acronym for *Employer Identification Number*, is a tax identifier issued by the IRS, which stands for the *Internal Revenue Service*. The IRS is the federal tax agency of the United States.

The EIN is issued to a U.S. company or to a non-American company doing business in the United States.

The EIN is issued on request only. So, it is not automatic. This request is usually made at the beginning of the company's existence.

This tax number is a sequence of nine digits, the first two being separated from the next seven by a hyphen.

OTHER NAMES

In popular language, the EIN is also known by various other names:

- FEIN, for *Federal Employer Identification Number*
- Tax ID, where *ID* stands for *Identification Document*
- Federal Tax ID
- TIN, for *Tax Identification Number*

USING THE EIN

The primary purpose of the EIN is to identify your company from a federal tax point of view. But in reality, this number is used by all levels of taxation in the United States:

- Federal
- State
- County
- City
- Etc.

In addition, the EIN is used by almost all participants in the U.S. financial system. For example, the EIN is essential for opening your company's bank account in the United States. Without this number, it is absolutely impossible to open a business bank account on U.S. soil. The situation is the same if you want to open a PayPal account for your company.

In short, the EIN is the equivalent, for a business, of the social security number for an individual.

Finally, here are three points you should remember.

1. ABSOLUTELY REQUIRED?

It is impossible for your company to do business in the United States without an EIN.

From a tax perspective, some American accountants and tax experts will tell you that this number is mandatory for corporations, but not necessarily for LLCs. The problem is that it is impossible for an LLC to open a bank account if it does not have an EIN. Therefore, this number is always requested for corporations and LLCs. On the other hand, it may happen that some LLCs, owned by foreigners, without a U.S. establishment and that do not do business on American soil, do not request the issuance of an EIN.

In any case, it is always advisable to consult a U.S. accountant or tax specialist to find out about your company's tax rights and obligations in the United States.

2. INVOICES

Contrary to what can be seen in Europe, it is rare that the EIN of a U.S. company is indicated on its invoices.

3. IDENTITY THEFT

There is more and more identity theft in the United States, even at the corporate level. In this context, it is quite surprising that the EIN of a company established in Florida is entered on the public register of that state.

7.2 - INCOME TAX

In the United States, there are several levels of corporate income tax.

First, there is the federal tax, which is applicable in all states.

Next, there is the state tax.

Forty-four states have an income tax ranging from 3% to 12% of net income.

Four states have no corporate income tax, but levy a tax on gross income, known as the *Gross Receipts Tax*. These states are:

- Nevada
- Ohio
- Texas
- Washington

Two states have no corporate income tax or gross receipts tax:

- Wyoming
- South Dakota

Finally, several counties, cities, and transportation commissions also have a corporate income tax.

For example, the City of Wilmington, Delaware, imposes the companies that are established there. The same is true for most cities in Pennsylvania.

U.S. corporate taxation is a very complex area. That is why the assistance of a tax professional or accountant is necessary for the well-being of your company in the United States.

7.3 - SALES TAX

In the United States, there is generally no federal sales tax.

However, the states have full jurisdiction to impose a sales tax.

STATES

Forty-five states and the District of Columbia, where the U.S. capital Washington is located, impose a sales tax. In 35 of these states, there are also local sales taxes, which are imposed by counties, cities, and transport commissions.

For example, in New York State, the same product is sold in four stores of the same chain, located in four different cities. Despite this, the combined sales tax rate may differ from one establishment to another.

COMBINED RATES

A table published on *taxfoundation.org* provides a comprehensive overview of combined sales tax rates in each state. Combined rates vary greatly from state to state. Moreover, these rates vary constantly over time, since they are regularly subject to change. The highest rate at the time of preparation of this table is 10.02% in Louisiana.

COMPARISON

To give you an idea of the sales tax situation in the United States, let us compare it with what is happening in other countries.

In France, there are some sales tax rates, the main one - TVA - being currently set at 20%.

In Canada, there are about ten sales tax rates, including the GST at the federal level, the QST in the province of Quebec, the HST in the other provinces, and some specific rates.

In the United States, if all levels of government that can impose a sales tax are taken into account, there would be more than 50,000 sales tax rates.

NO SALES TAX

Finally, five states do not impose any sales tax:

- Alaska
- Delaware
- Montana
- New Hampshire
- Oregon

In addition, none of these states allows cities and localities in its territory to impose a sales tax, except Alaska and Montana.

7.4 - TAX TREATIES

A tax treaty is essentially an agreement between two countries. Therefore, there is normally no possibility of a tax treaty between, for example, Belgium and Delaware.

TAX CONSEQUENCES

This agreement between two countries deals with tax consequences resulting from various situations that may arise as a result of the fact or action of a natural or legal person. For example, what happens if an individual residing in France earns copyright income from a U.S. company? Are copyrights taxable in the United States, France, both countries, or neither country? The purpose of the tax treaty is to resolve these types of issues. This means that a tax treaty may, in effect, change one or more provisions of the tax law of either of the two countries concerned.

STATES

On the other hand, since states are not parties to any tax treaty signed by the United States, they have no obligation to comply with it. Tax treaties only bind the U.S. federal government and other signatory countries.

Finally, here are three points you should remember.

1. WORLDWIDE INCOME

According to accountants and tax experts, your U.S. corporation generally has to file a tax return, at least at the federal level, and pay taxes in the United States on its worldwide income. Even if it does not have a physical establishment in the United States, even if it does not do business on U.S. soil, and even if it has no shareholder, director, officer, or employee in that country, your corporation must still file a U.S. tax return on its worldwide income.

The tax situation of your LLC may be different, often even advantageous. But this can depend on many factors. A tax specialist or accountant specializing in U.S. taxation will be able to provide you with adequate information on this subject.

2. PHYSICAL IMPLANTATION

If you want to physically establish your company's operations in the United States, there is not necessarily an ideal location. Each state has its advantages and disadvantages. Before choosing one state over another, you must analyze everything. Not just the tax rate or the sales tax rate. A multitude of factors must be considered before making your choice, including the following:

- Availability of manpower
- Land, rail, and air transport facilities
- Proximity to customers
- Proximity to suppliers and subcontractors

- Quality of life
- Subsidies
- Taxation

There are several companies that offer professional analysis and location research services in the United States.

3. DELAWARE

If you create a corporation in the State of Delaware and it has no physical presence, it generally does not pay any taxes in Delaware. However, if you create a corporation in the State of Florida, it must file a tax return in Florida, simply because it was created in that state. Often, the best choice for companies planning to operate virtually or have multiple offices in the United States is to create a company in the State of Delaware.

8 - SOME CORPORATE SITUATIONS

8.1 - AUTHORIZATION TO DO BUSINESS IN ANOTHER STATE

If your company was created in any state, it normally has the right to do business there. For example, your company ABC Inc. was created in Delaware. It can therefore carry out business activities without delay. But if your Delaware company wants to open a store in Florida, it will need to get permission from that state to do business there.

FOREIGN COMPANY

In the United States, any company that has not been created in a particular state is considered a foreign company.

For example, your company ABC Inc. was created in Delaware. For Delaware, ABC Inc. is a domestic company because it was established in that state.

Now, ABC Inc. wants to do business in Florida. For Florida, ABC Inc. is a foreign company because it was not created in that state. If it had been created in Florida, then we would be talking about a domestic company. It is the same situation all over the United States.

A foreign company can be a company created not only outside the state, but also outside the United States.

For example, your French company wants to establish an office in California. For California purposes, your French company is considered a foreign company. In other words, it is a foreign company in California. So, for this state, as for all others, there is no difference between a company created in Delaware and a company created in France: these two companies are considered foreign entities.

The definition of *doing business* varies from state to state. There are therefore several situations requiring state authorization. Here are some of them:

PHYSICAL BUSINESS PLACE

Your company ABC Inc., created in Delaware, wants to establish a physical business location in Florida. A physical place of business generally refers to a store, office, warehouse, or showroom. ABC Inc. will therefore have to obtain authorization from the State of Florida to do business there.

EMPLOYEE

ABC Inc. wishes to hire an employee to work in Texas, either from home or from any other location in that state. ABC Inc. will be presumed to do business in Texas through that employee. Your company will therefore have to obtain Texas' authorization to do business there.

REGULAR BUSINESS

ABC Inc. regularly signs contracts, makes regular sales, or performs regular services in the State of Illinois. It will therefore normally be presumed to do business there, and consequently, will need to obtain the required authorization from Illinois.

AMOUNT OF SALES

ABC Inc. sells products and services for $2.3 million annually to California residents. It will be presumed to do business there simply because of its annual amount of sales. It will therefore have to ask permission from that state to do business there.

ADMINISTRATIVE AUTHORIZATION

The authorization to do business in a state is not a discretionary but rather an administrative authorization. If you meet the required criteria, the state has no choice but to grant you this permission. Anyway, states are always happy to welcome new taxpayers!

Finally, here are three points you should remember.

1. TAXATION

Attention must be paid to the tax consequences of applying for authorization to do business in a state. Upon obtaining this authorization, your company automatically enters the tax system of the state concerned.

2. NAME AVAILABILITY

What happens if the name of your company ABC Inc. created in Delaware is not available in Florida? Indeed, as we know, there are 50 states as well as the District of Columbia, so 51 places where a company can be created. There may well be your company ABC Inc. established in Delaware and another company ABC Inc. established in Florida by a third party.

In such a case, your Delaware-based ABC Inc. may still obtain authorization to do business in Florida, but under a name other than its own. It must then use what is called an assumed name. For example, this assumed name may be *ABC Inc. of Delaware*. In such a case, the Florida business register will show two names:

- ABC Inc., a domestic company — created in Florida
- ABC Inc. of Delaware, a foreign company — created in Delaware

3. REGISTERED AGENT

A company seeking authorization to do business in a state other than the one in which it was created must retain the services of a registered agent in that state. In the previous example, your company ABC Inc. has a registered agent in Delaware. Since your company has obtained authorization to do business in Florida, it also has a registered agent in Florida.

At CorpoMax, some of our Delaware-based customers' companies operate in over 40 states. These companies therefore have at least 40 registered agents - members of our national network - plus CorpoMax, who represents them as a registered agent in Delaware.

8.2 - ASSUMED NAME

An assumed name is a business name under which a company does business, and which is a name other than its legal name. For example, your company ABC Inc. operates under the name *Gogopro*. In the United States, we say *doing business as* or its acronym *DBA*:

- ABC Inc. doing business as Gogopro
- ABC Inc. dba Gogopro

DESIGNATIONS

According to the states, there are various names to designate the same thing:

- Alias Name
- Assumed Name
- Business Name
- DBA Name
- Fictitious Name
- Trade Name

Under what circumstances will your U.S. company want or need to use an assumed name?

COMMERCIAL ESTABLISHMENT

First, your company ABC Inc. may want to use an assumed name in connection with the operation of its restaurant known as *Gogopro*.

It can, therefore, file an application to register the name *Gogopro*, provided that it is available.

MERCHANT ACCOUNT

A company may also want to use an assumed name in connection with the operation of its website. For example, ABC Inc. has an online store called *Pitago*. Visitors to the website can make purchases using their credit card.

When these visitors, who become buyers, then receive their credit card statement, they expect to see *Pitago* in connection with their purchase and not ABC Inc.

ANOTHER STATE

A company may also be forced to use an assumed name in a state other than the one in which it was created.

For example, if the name of your Delaware-based company ABC Inc. is not available in Florida, it can do business there under the name *ABC Inc. of Delaware* or it may also adopt a completely different name, like *Ritalo Inc.*, if this name is available in Florida.

SPECIFIC DIVISION

Finally, a company may also wish to do business under another name, especially to identify a specific division of its business. For example, ABC Inc. may want to do business under the assumed name *Botino* to identify one of its divisions.

Finally, here are three points you should remember.

1. LEGAL IDENTIFIER

An assumed name cannot usually contain a legal identifier, such as *Inc.* or *LLC*.

An exception to this rule is registration in another state, where the name of your company is not available. For example, your Delaware company ABC Inc. may be listed on the Florida Register as *ABC Inc. of Delaware*.

However, other states do not allow this. For example, your Delaware company ABC Inc. may be listed on the New York State Register under *ABC of Delaware* - without the identifier *Inc.*

2. REGISTRATION

The procedures for registering an assumed name vary from state to state. For example, in Florida, the registration of an assumed name is done at the state level. However, in Delaware, the registration of the assumed name is done at the level of one or more of its three counties - New Castle County, Kent County, and Sussex County.

3. PROTECTION

According to several lawyers, the protection afforded by an assumed name is minimal. In some states or counties, it is even non-existent. According to these lawyers, this is probably the worst form of protection for a business name. Moreover, this protection - however minimal - is valid only in the state or county in which the assumed name has been registered. Instead, lawyers generally recommend filing a federal trademark application, which provides protection throughout the United States.

8.3 - CONVERSION AND DOMESTICATION

Let us now look at what it means to convert or domesticate a company.

It is usually possible to convert a corporation into an LLC, or an LLC into a corporation. Indeed, there may be various reasons for a company to change its legal form.

TAX BENEFITS

Sometimes, a company's legal form can confer significant tax advantages, in particular following a legislative amendment. In such a case, it can sometimes be advantageous to change the legal form of your U.S. company.

In such a case, it can sometimes be advantageous to change the legal form of your U.S. company.

ERROR

It may happen that an error was made when creating the legal entity. You have created a corporation, when in fact, it would have been better to create an LLC. In such a case, a request can be made for your corporation to be converted to an LLC.

MERGER OR ACQUISITION

Another reason for conversion is the desire to harmonize the legal form of companies involved in a merger or acquisition.

For example, an LLC wishes to convert to a corporation before merging with another corporation.

It is also possible to domesticate a foreign company into a domestic company. For example, your corporation created in Florida wishes to continue its existence under Delaware corporate law, and therefore be domesticated as a Delaware domestic corporation. As we have seen previously, a foreign company is a legal entity that was created in another state or country.

Again, there are several reasons why a foreign company may domesticate itself into a domestic company in a particular state.

RELOCATION OF THE HEAD OFFICE

For example, a California-based company decides to move its head office to the state of Maine. Its directors may decide to domesticate the Californian company so that it becomes a domestic company in Maine.

ACQUISITION OF A NON-U.S. COMPANY

Often, business leaders want all companies in their group to be governed by the same corporate laws. For example, your Delaware company acquires a Canadian corporation, with the intention of relocating its operations to the United States. In such a case, a request will be made for the Canadian corporation to be domesticated as a Delaware company.

LEGISLATION

In some circumstances, the corporate law of one state may be more advantageous than that of another state. In such a case, domestication may be considered.

MERGER

Sometimes, domestication facilitates the merger of companies from different jurisdictions. For example, an Oregon corporation and your Delaware company want to merge, and then want the merged company to be governed by Delaware corporate laws. In such a case, the Oregon company can first be domesticated as a Delaware company. Subsequently, the two Delaware companies can easily merge.

The conversion or domestication of your company can have significant legal, accounting, and tax consequences. Therefore, it is strongly recommended to consult professionals specialized in this field.

9 - CLOSING YOUR COMPANY

9.1. - VOLUNTARY DISSOLUTION

The directors of a U.S. company sometimes have to make the decision to cease business operations.

In such a case, they generally liquidate the assets and dissolve the company.

Here are some reasons that may lead to the dissolution of your company.

BUSINESS PROBLEMS

Losing a major customer, a large contract, or a key employee can sometimes cause your company to close its doors.

A disaster - such as fire or theft - can also have disastrous consequences.

TAX CHANGES

Some changes in tax legislation can sometimes be detrimental to your company and lead to its closure. For example, the cost of products sold by your company is no longer eligible for a tax deduction for its customers.

DEATH

The death of the company's founder or a key employee can sometimes lead to the company's dissolution.

LEGAL PROCEEDINGS

The fact that your company is being sued in court may also lead to its closure, and therefore to its dissolution. Indeed, the legal costs of defending oneself are generally high in the United States. On the other hand, a judgment with a large monetary conviction can also cause your company to shut down.

INTRA-CORPORATE CONFLICT

A disagreement between the shareholders, directors, or officers of your company on the business vision or conduct of the company can sometimes lead to its dissolution. This is even more true when the two leaders of the company, who are also spouses in everyday life, decide to divorce. In either case, if there is no possible agreement between the parties, dissolution is often the best solution.

CERTIFICATE OF DISSOLUTION

The dissolution process generally ends with the issuance of a state certificate confirming the dissolution of your company. Again, several names are possible for this document, depending on the issuing state and type of legal entity:

- Articles of Cancellation
- Articles of Dissolution
- Certificate of Cancellation
- Certificate of Dissolution
- Certificate of Termination
- Certificate of Termination of Existence
- Statement of Dissolution
- Statement of Termination

Finally, here are three points you should remember.

1. INACTION

The worst thing to do when your U.S. company stops business is to do nothing from a corporate point of view. American lawyers invariably recommend that you quickly dissolve your company, especially if it has been assigned an EIN tax number.

2. LIABILITY

In the United States, there are reportedly more than 5,000 laws providing for personal action against directors or officers of a company. Most of these laws provide for a limitation period for legal actions that may be brought against company representatives. U.S. lawyers again recommend that you immediately dissolve your company when it ceases to operate.

3. CHECKS

Before dissolving your company and closing its bank account, you must ensure that all checks you expect have been cashed. For example, you are expecting a tax refund check from the IRS. If you close your company's bank account too quickly, you will no longer be able to cash a check made payable to it. On the other hand, once dissolved, your company will no longer be able to open a bank account.

9.2 - FORCED DISSOLUTION

Here are the main reasons that could lead to the forced dissolution of your U.S. company.

ANNUAL REPORT

If your company fails to file its annual report with the state for a period of two years, the company will generally be dissolved under the law. However, it is usually possible to revive a company that has been administratively dissolved, by paying government fees, as well as penalties and interest. In some states, it is no longer possible to revive a company after a certain period of time following the date of administrative dissolution.

ANNUAL TAX

If your company fails to pay the annual tax to the state, this can lead to its administrative dissolution, usually after two years.

REGISTERED AGENT

If your company fails to pay the fees of its registered agent in the state where it was created or in the state where it does business, that agent may then resign. If the resigning agent is not replaced by another agent within the time limit prescribed by law - for example, 30 days - this usually results in an automatic dissolution of the company by the state.

SHAREHOLDER

If minority shareholders feel their rights have been violated, they can ask the courts to dissolve your company. This situation can also occur if there is a deadlock between two equal shareholders.

CREDITOR

Finally, an unpaid creditor may ask the courts to order the dissolution of your company if it has failed to pay the claim.

In either case, an American lawyer specializing in corporate law will be able to advise you properly.

10 - CONCLUSION

10.1 - THE ABCS OF DOING BUSINESS IN THE UNITED STATES

Do you know the ABCs of doing business in the United States?

It is very easy to remember.

A IS FOR *ATTORNEY*

A lawyer specializing in American corporate law can guide you in choosing the legal structure and the most appropriate jurisdiction for the creation of your company. The lawyer then prepares the incorporation documents and normally gives you a binder containing the official certificates and corporate documents ready for signature.

But you can also do business directly with a company specializing in corporate services. Moreover, several lawyers often retain the services of these specialized companies, under contract.

If you are a foreign entrepreneur, a U.S. immigration attorney can help you in many aspects of setting up your business. Remember that the mere fact of creating a company does not automatically imply the right to immigrate to or work in the United States. The lawyer can assist you on several levels.

For example, they can advise you on obtaining a work visa for you and your employees. They can also guide you through the process of immigrating legally to the United States and obtaining a permanent residence card, commonly known as a *Green Card.* The attorney can also advise you on customs clearance, the information you need to provide to the customs officers and the documents you need to submit, if needed.

There are several gateways to the United States. You have to choose the right one, the one that will be the most appropriate for your situation. A word of advice: do not try to do this without the assistance of a lawyer! You may think that these are just simple forms to fill out. The reality is totally different. An experienced lawyer will be an essential guide in your approach.

A lawyer specialized in real estate law can assist you in the acquisition or rental of a building or commercial space. Please note that there is no notary in the United States, in the European or Quebec sense of the term. So, a lawyer will proceed with the transaction.

Finally, an intellectual property attorney can be a good advisor for the protection of your company's trademarks, patents, industrial designs, and copyrights.

B IS FOR *BANKER*

Generally, a U.S. company needs a U.S. bank account. However, you must understand that since September 11, 2001, the banking reality in the United States has changed significantly. Today, bankers open bank accounts and compliance departments are likely to close them shortly thereafter. This is why it is often recommended to have a bank account in two different banks.

C IS FOR *CERTIFIED PUBLIC ACCOUNTANT*

I should also add a tax expert. In the United States, the tax expert is often a certified public accountant, unlike in some other countries, where the tax professional is rather a lawyer.

The accountant or tax specialist specializing in American taxation is of crucial importance. As we have seen previously, U.S. taxation is very complex. In this sense, a CPA or tax expert is undoubtedly the most important professional. However, if you are a foreign entrepreneur, it is recommended to choose an accountant or tax expert who is fully familiar with the tax treaty between the United States and your country of residence. Indeed, a purely American accountant, used to serving only Americans, will not generally be of much help to you. So, if you live outside the United States, it is often recommended to retain the services of an accountant or tax specialist who specializes in U.S. taxation and practices in your country of residence.

There are also other professionals who are very helpful.

CUSTOMS BROKERS

Among them are customs brokers. Firms specializing in international transport - such as FedEx, UPS, and DHL - offer customs brokerage services.

IMPORT-EXPORT CONSULTANTS

There are also advisers on the import and export of products and services. These can provide you with a wealth of useful information. Their contact list is often impressive. Several governmental agencies also provide advice and assistance in this regard.

EMBASSIES AND CONSULATES

In addition, American embassies and consulates in your country or your country's embassies and consulates in the United States can be of great help. They often keep a list of lawyers, accountants, and tax specialists who can assist you in an appropriate way.

REAL ESTATE BROKERS

Other important stakeholders include real estate brokers. Before buying or renting a building in the United States, it is important to know the area involved. Often, it is preferable to rent before acquiring a building. This allows you to discover your new environment and analyze its advantages and disadvantages.

INSURANCE BROKERS

The important professionals obviously include insurance brokers. These are often specialized in a particular field:

- Automobile Insurance
- Damage Insurance
- Disability Insurance
- Health Insurance
- Liability Insurance
- Life Insurance

WEBSITES

Finally, several websites can provide you with valuable information. These include government websites, both American and those in your country. There are also specialized websites that offer significant resources and advice. In addition, YouTube contains several informative videos.

Finally, here are three points you should remember.

1. LANGUAGE AND ACCENT

If you are a foreign entrepreneur, do not worry about your knowledge of English or your accent in that language.

Since 2001, CorpoMax has helped thousands of entrepreneurs from more than 50 countries launch their American business. Several expressed concern about the language barrier. Others were concerned about their pronounced accent in English.

Remember one thing. The United States is a country of immigrants. They have millions of ways of speaking English, with millions of different accents. As an American once told me when I immigrated to the United States in 1999, "*... the important thing is that we understand you and that you understand us.*"

So do not worry about your knowledge of English or your accent. Go for it!

2. BEST TIMING

Do not wait for the best timing to launch your American company. The best moment is now.

On September 1, 2001, CorpoMax opened its doors. Ten days later, on September 11, the earth stopped turning.

During the next six months, CorpoMax had no customers, no phone calls, no emails, no orders, no income. I could have cried or just closed the books. Instead, I took the opportunity to improve the new

CorpoMax website and to deepen my knowledge of creating companies in the United States. Today, almost 20 years later, CorpoMax has several thousand customers operating in more than 50 countries.

I repeat: the best moment is now!

3. ENTREPRENEUR

To be an entrepreneur is to undertake. To undertake is to begin.

Yes, there will be obstacles. Yes, there will be problems. Yes, there will be disappointments. But that is part of an entrepreneur's life.

Think that it will be the sum of your efforts that will ensure that your American company can prosper. Also, consider that you are about to embark on an exciting adventure that will bring you great knowledge and immense satisfaction.

The United States is an extraordinary country for entrepreneurs. I have lived here since 1999. As an entrepreneur, I live the American dream every day. Now it is up to you to live the American dream. And you do not even need to live in this country to experience it.

~

If you enjoyed this practical guide, feel free to post a comment on the website where you got it.

If you have any questions, comments, or suggestions, please do not hesitate to contact me.

Thank you and good luck in your American adventure!

USEFUL RESOURCES

You will find the list of useful resources at:

www.corpomax.com/start

This list of useful resources is constantly updated and enriched, especially by your contributions.

If you discover a site or a web page that should be in this list, please do not hesitate to send me the web link.

In addition, if any of the links on this list are broken, please let me know.

Happy surfing!

ACKNOWLEDGMENTS

I would like to sincerely thank:

- My wife **Sylvie DUSSAULT ALLARD**, Director of Customer Service at CorpoMax, who always shares my creative and literary impulses - often in spite of herself
- My son **Jérémie ALLARD**, who meticulously revised the English version of the three practical guides, in addition to being the narrator in their audio version
- My stepdaughter **Véronique ALLARD**, Managing Director at CorpoMax, with whom I have had the pleasure of working for more than 10 years
- My friend **Marie-Andrée LEMIEUX**, highly talented artist, who has been taking care of my imaging and graphic design needs since 1995
- My colleague **Bettina KARPEL**, lawyer and legal translator, who has been working on my translation needs since 1995
- My friend **Christine BUREAU**, virtual collaborator and responsible for the launch of the practical guides in the *Yes to Entrepreneurs®* series

ABOUT VINCENT ALLARD

Since 1981, Vincent Allard has been a lawyer and a member of the Quebec Bar. He is also a member of the Canadian Bar Association and the American Bar Association.

He holds three university degrees:

- Law degree - LL.L. - from University of Montréal
- Master of Business Law - LL.M. - University of Ottawa, Canada
- Master of Business Administration - MBA - from École des HEC in Montreal, Canada.

For 18 years, Vincent Allard practiced business law, including corporate law and commercial litigation, primarily as a founding partner of the Pigeon, Allard law firm in Montreal.

In 1995, he co-founded Jurifax (jurifax.com), a legal publishing company that distributes more than 600 legal forms and other legal products via the Internet.

In 2001, shortly after emigrating to the United States, he founded CorpoMax (corpomax.com). Located in the state of Delaware, CorpoMax offers U.S. company formation and U.S. trademark services to thousands of entrepreneurs and professionals working in more than 50 countries.

In 2017, he launched DictoMax (dictomax.com), which offers online training to entrepreneurs and professionals.

In 2020, Vincent Allard published three practical guides for entrepreneurs:

- In English and French
- In digital, paperback, and audio formats
- All part of the *Yes to Entrepreneurs®* series.

For more than 15 years, Vincent Allard has provided training on the organization and launch of companies in the United States, mainly to foreign entrepreneurs, lawyers, accountants and tax specialists.

TO CONTACT VINCENT ALLARD

- Email: vallard@corpomax.com
- Phone: +1 302 266 8200
- Skype: corpomax

linkedin.com/in/corpomax
twitter.com/corpomax
youtube.com/corpomax
facebook.com/corpomax

BOOKS BY VINCENT ALLARD

www.corpomax.com/practical-guides

How to Start Your Business in the United States

Create Your U.S. Company

in Delaware or Elsewhere in the USA

How to Name Your Business in the United States

Find and Protect the Name of Your Company

in the United States and Abroad

How to Open Your Bank Account in the United States

Open and Manage Your

Business or Personal Account in the USA

Ces livres sont aussi disponibles en français :

www.corpomax.com/guides-pratiques

LEGAL INFORMATION

This practical guide contains a lot of information available on the Internet from public sources. However, it is by no means a legal, accounting or tax guide. Therefore, you should be well aware that this guide does not provide legal, accounting or tax advice. To obtain such advice, tailored to your particular situation, you must therefore contact a lawyer, accountant or tax expert working in the appropriate jurisdiction.

Every effort has been made to make this guide as complete and accurate as possible. Although the author and the publisher have prepared this guide with the greatest of care, and have made every effort to ensure the accuracy, they assume no responsibility or liability for errors, inaccuracies, or omissions. Before you begin, check with the appropriate authorities to ensure compliance with all laws and regulations.

On the other hand, this guide may contain mistakes in typography or content. Also, this guide contains information valid only until the date of its publication.

Therefore, this practical guide should be used as a guide only - not as the ultimate source of information. The purpose of this guide is for educational purposes only. The author and the publisher do not warrant that the information contained in this guide is fully complete and shall not be responsible for any errors or omissions. The author and the publisher shall have neither liability nor responsibility to any person or entity with respect to any loss or damage caused or alleged to be caused directly or indirectly by this guide, nor do they make any claims or promises of your ability to generate income by using any of the information contained in this guide.

Finally, the list of useful resources, which is offered as a bonus with this guide, contains a series of hyperlinks, which are provided for informational purposes only. The author and the publisher do not guarantee that the information contained in the websites concerned by these hyperlinks is complete, adequate or truthful. Therefore, the author and the publisher incur no liability to any person or entity for any loss or damage caused or suspected to be caused directly or indirectly by the use of the information contained in one or more of the websites concerned. The author and publisher make no representation or promise of your ability to generate income by using the information contained in one or more of the relevant websites.

Made in the USA
Las Vegas, NV
17 January 2026

39597628R00094